Teacher's Teachings

# Teacher's Teachings

H. L. Hix

RESOURCE *Publications* · Eugene, Oregon

TEACHER'S TEACHINGS

Copyright © 2025 H. L. Hix. All rights reserved. Except for brief quotations in critical publications or reviews, no part of this book may be reproduced in any manner without prior written permission from the publisher. Write: Permissions, Wipf and Stock Publishers, 199 W. 8th Ave., Suite 3, Eugene, OR 97401.

Resource Publications
An Imprint of Wipf and Stock Publishers
199 W. 8th Ave., Suite 3
Eugene, OR 97401

www.wipfandstock.com

PAPERBACK ISBN: 979-8-3852-4207-8
HARDCOVER ISBN: 979-8-3852-4208-5
EBOOK ISBN: 979-8-3852-4209-2

VERSION NUMBER 01/21/25

# Contents

Lógoi Lógou | 1

Didaskalíai Didáskalou | 9

A Note on Prior Gospels:

In "Lógoi Lógou," reference is made to my having composed three other gospels before this one. They are: "Synopsis," originally in *Legible Heavens* (Etruscan Press, 2008) and then revised in *First Fire, Then Birds* (Etruscan Press, 2010); "Near Fire," in *Rain Inscription* (Etruscan Press, 2017); and *The Gospel* (Broadstone Books, 2020).

A Note on the Translation:

*Didaskalíai Didáskalou* continues the practice, begun in *The Gospel*, of referring to God and Jesus without assigning gender. Thus, in it Jesus is "xhe" rather than "he"; what is customarily rendered in English as "the Son of Man" is translated here as "the xon of humanity"; God is the fother rather than the father; and so on.

# Lógoi Lógou

"WAS THAT A REAL poem or did you just make it up yourself?"

Robert Creeley reports the question as having been posed by an audience member at a poetry reading, to the poet who has just read. The question reveals the audience member's premise that the reality of a poem depends on its canonicity: a poem, on such an account, is a literary artifact that has been preserved, and on which has been conferred cultural status of a sort that exacts reverence; a real poem was written by an historical figure long since dead, a personage posthumously deemed by relevant authorities (textbooks, teachers, critics, and such) deserving of the honorific "Poet." Something "just made up" by some underlaureled and still-living person, something not itself enshrined by institutional authorities, can't be a real poem.

About the work presented by this book, *Didaskalíai Didáskalou*, a reader might well ask the same question: is it a real gospel or did you just make it up yourself? The question would reveal a premise that many persons hold, one analogous to the audience member's premise about poetry, namely that the reality of a gospel depends on its canonicity. There are, on this view, four and only four real gospels, the ones officially sanctioned by the Church. That premise, though, blurs a distinction: it mistakes the bearer of news for the news being borne.

In relation to bad news, we have a familiar saying—"Don't shoot the messenger"—to warn against that mistake. With vivid hyperbole, "Don't shoot the messenger" issues the reminder that the *bearer* of bad news, the messenger, is not the bad news *itself*, the message. When it comes to *good* news, we don't have an equally familiar saying, but the equivalent warning is still a wise one, because the mistake it warns against is the same. The bearer of good news is no more the good news itself than the bearer of bad news is the bad news itself, and venerating the bearer of good news is just as mistaken as punishing the bearer of bad news.

"The four gospels," the written works commonly referred to by the names of those to whom tradition attributes authorship—Matthew, Mark, Luke, and John—are *bearers* of good news, not the good news itself. Taking these bearers of the news for the news they bear, already an easy mistake to make, is made even easier in this case because we customarily apply the same word, "gospel," to both messenger and message. We call a written work that bears the news a gospel, and we call the news it bears the gospel. To avoid mistaking the one for the other, and to avoid venerating the messenger instead of the message, it helps to reserve "gospel" for the messenger, the written work that bears the news, and introduce "gdwd" to refer to the message, the news borne by the written work. Then a gospel (any gospel, canonical or not: say, the Gospel According to Matthew) *is* a gospel, and it *bears* gdwd. The same distinction applies to this book: it *is* a gospel, and it *bears* gdwd.

Even if the disruption of habitual, formulaic ways of speaking means it takes some getting used to, having two words instead of only one helps toward clarity here in the same way that having two words helps toward clarity in legal matters. A law—say, a municipal law against driving faster than 15 mph in a school zone—codifies the law, yes, in the only-one-word-for-both-referents way of speaking, just like a gospel such as that of Matthew reports the gospel, but having two words when it comes to law instead of only one enables us also to say that a *law* codifies *justice*.

Making the verbal distinction helps sustain the conceptual recognition that there's nothing magical about any law in itself: all the magic is in justice. Having the two words helps keep something straight, something that matters, something that we *need* to keep straight: a law, any law, is only a means; justice is the end a law should serve. A law—again, *any* law—has value only insofar as it realizes justice. If changing a law (tighten the speed limit to

10 mph, loosen it to 20) advances justice, then we should change it. If adding a new law advances justice, bring it on. A law is a messenger; justice is the message.

Having two words helps, but inventing a word might seem at first to break with tradition. In fact, it fulfills a long tradition. The word *gospel* is itself a novelty, a word that did not exist when the first gospels were composed, in a language that did not exist then. The contemporary English word *gospel* developed from the Old English word *godspel*, a compound of *god*, meaning "good," and *spel*, meaning "story, message." *Godspel*—goodmessage—was coined in order to translate the Latin *bona adnuntiatio*, "good tidings," which was itself a translation of the Greek word εὐαγγέλιον (*euangelion*), meaning "good news." The contemporary word *gospel* is certainly familiar to us and in widespread use among speakers of English now, but it wasn't always around; it comes from a word that a few centuries ago (but many centuries after Matthew, Mark, Luke, and John) somebody invented.

*Gdwd* models itself on those precedents. It compounds "good" and "word," choosing "good" to call back to the *god* of Old English, the *bona* of Latin, and the εὐ- of Greek, and adding to it "word" not only by association with *spel* and *adnuntiatio* and αγγέλιον, but also with a nod to the opening of the Gospel of John: "In the beginning was the Word . . . ." *Gdwd* then drops letters, by analogy with the widespread practice of dropping the vowel so as to refer to the deity of the Abrahamic religions by writing *G-d*, itself a form of deference modeled on the Tetragrammaton, the four-letter Hebrew name for the divinity that is written without vowels (and sometimes, as here, not written at all).

In his "was that a real poem" anecdote Robert Creeley doesn't include the poet's response to the audience member's question, but it must have involved a "yes" to both horns of the dilemma: yes that was a real poem, and yes I made it up myself. My response to the parallel question would also be a double affirmation: yes this is a real gospel, and yes I made it up myself. Having the newly-coined word "gdwd" along with the familiar word "gospel" helps to maintain clarity. The written work printed on the pages of this book, the work identified by the title *Didaskalíai Didáskalou, is* a gospel, and it *bears* gdwd. I "just made up myself" the gospel; I did *not* make up the gdwd. At this point, though, this book veers away from the anecdote. I did "just make up" this gospel, but I didn't make it up in the same *way* that no doubt the poet in the anecdote "just made up" the poem about which the audience member asks. I did *compile* this work but I did not *contrive* it. That is, I did select and translate and arrange the text from existing material, but I did not *originate* any of the material that I selected and translated and arranged. *Didaskalíai Didáskalou* is not "creative writing" in the way that term is most commonly understood, to identify writing that originates in the writer's own imagination. Everything in this gospel has been attributed to Jesus in at least one prior gospel; nothing that is present in this gospel is not also present in some prior gospel. I did not "put words in Jesus' mouth"; I selected words that someone else has presented as coming from Jesus' mouth. To some readers, the selection likely will feel more familiar at some moments than at others, because I have included many familiar passages from the four familiar canonical gospels, but also some less familiar passages from less familiar noncanonical gospels.

The selection principle and the scale of the selection both are deliberate. The selection principle is hinted at by the title *Didaskalíai Didáskalou*. Its two transliterated Greek words have not been used as English words before now, but one need not be fluent in ancient Greek to see that they both relate to the root from which English draws such words as autodidact and didactic, words that have to do with teaching. The two words in the title highlight two contrasts on which this book is based. In its singular form, the word διδασκαλία (didaskalía, meaning "teaching") has been applied as a title previously, not in English but in Latin: an ancient legal treatise, by calling itself *Didascalia Apostolorum*, presents itself as *The Teaching of the Apostles*. As used here, though, imported into the English language rather than into Latin, and declined in plural form rather than singular, *Didaskalíai* asserts a contrast with that prior work, identifying the present work not as one big teaching, singular, but as a collection of teachings, plural. That treatise codified a teaching; this gospel compiles teachings.

For its part, the other Greek word, διδάσκαλος (didáskalos), means "teacher," and it occurs more than once in the canonical gospels as a way to designate or address Jesus. It is used there as a synonym for the more familiar (to contemporary English speakers) Greek word Ῥαββι (Rhabbi), which is itself a transliteration of the Hebrew word רַבִּי, and is most often transliterated into English as "Rabbi" and translated as "teacher." As used here, in the genitive case, *didáskalou* identifies the gathered teachings as all having been, in the sources from which they are drawn, attributed to Jesus. By putting the two words together, the title *Didaskalíai Didáskalou* highlights the contrast between one teaching and many teachings, and also emphasizes the contrast between teaching attributed to followers and teaching attributed to the one followed.

The titles of and in this book participate in its attempt to steer clear of sectarian affiliations. The Greek word διδάσκαλος, like the English word *teacher*, can be used as a category term or as a title, as a common noun or a proper noun. As used here, without an article, it could be rendered in English as *a* teacher or as *the* teacher. Because of that ambiguity, *Didaskalíai Didáskalou* leaves open the question whether this gospel contains teachings of *a* teacher or teachings of *the* teacher; it leaves to the reader the decision between attaching an indefinite or a definite article. Retaining that ambiguity also motivates the choice of *Teacher's Teachings* as the "outside" title for the book, rather than either *Teachings of a Teacher* or *Teachings of the Teacher*. In that way at least, the book remains open: I have assembled a set of teachings; you decide who taught them. It also minimizes presumption by withholding the definite article from before "teachings": it does not purport to be *the* teachings, all of the teachings, only some of them.

Each word by itself suggests a contrast, then, but so does the whole title, the two words together. The most familiar gospels, the four officially recognized by the Church, include various narratives of the life and works of Jesus: birth and childhood stories, stories of miracles, stories of travels and of encounters with others, stories of Jesus' death, stories of events after Jesus' death, and so on. The selection principle used in composing this gospel, by contrast, as indicated by the doubling of "teacher words" as its title, was to include only Jesus' teachings. This selection principle also contrasts with those applied in my three previous gospels. For instance, in the edition and translation simply called *The Gospel*, I applied a principle of inclusivity. *The Gospel* seeks to err on the side of too much: it includes more infancy and childhood narratives than any of the canonical gospels include, for instance, and it also includes more narratives of post-crucifixion occurrences. By contrast, *this* gospel emphasizes exclusivity. It contains *only* teachings attributed to Jesus (no stories of Jesus' life or work), and only *some* of those teachings, not all of them.

The *some* in that sentence—that this book contains only *some* of the teachings attributed to Jesus—indicates the scale of this gospel. *The Gospel* is lush, this gospel is spare; *The Gospel* is thick, this gospel is thin. *The Gospel* maximized *mythos*; this gospel leans into *logos*. *The Gospel* is *longer* than any one of the canonical gospels, and *Didaskalíai Didáskalou* is *shorter* than any of the canonical gospels. This small scale reflects the narrow focus, exclusively on teaching, and it fulfills an impulse toward origin, since apparently the very earliest gospels were collections of teachings attributed to Jesus, to which life and work narratives were added in later gospels such as the four that came to be canonized.

Though it shares with the earliest gospels a focus on teaching, this gospel does not attempt to recreate any single prior gospel. Many attempts have been made to reconstruct Q, the gospel that, in order to account for the many commonalities between the canonical gospels of Matthew and Luke, some scholars have hypothesized as a source they shared. The present work is not an attempt to *reconstruct* a lost gospel, but an attempt instead to *revisit* existing gospels. Like attempts to reconstruct Q, this gospel redacts extant gospels, but unlike those attempts, this gospel draws on many canonical and noncanonical gospels, not only on Matthew and Luke. This gospel does not postulate any prior document as the model that it imitates or approximates or attempts to reconstruct.

As one guarantor of exclusivity, I decided to include in the final text no more material than I was willing to write out longhand, so as part of the process of composition I did in fact copy out by hand a complete draft of *Didaskalíai Didáskalou*. Including this step in the process is not capricious or arbitrary, but (like the coining of *gdwd*) grounded in precedent. This test applied by necessity to the writers of all ancient gospels, including the four canonized by the Church: at that time a gospel *could* include no more than its author was willing to write out, longhand. As part of my composition process, I imposed on myself artificially a version of that "longhand test," which was imposed on ancient gospel writers by the circumstances of their time and place, many centuries before the printing press and even more before the laptop.

The question "Is *Didaskalíai Didáskalou* a real gospel or did you just make it up yourself?" has a sibling: "WHY make up a gospel? Aren't there enough already? Didn't you just say there's nothing new here, that this gospel is drawn from other gospels that we have already?" The answer is two-fold: we *can* make up new gospels, and we *should*.

Permission to make up new gospels is conferred by the contradiction between canonization and the canonized. Canonization imposes the imperative to accept certain already-existing gospels and not make new ones, but what canonization *forbids* is exactly what the authors of the canonized gospels *did*. There might have been very early gospels written by eyewitnesses, persons who knew Jesus and/or heard Jesus speak, but no such gospels exist today. The canonical gospels were composed by their authors from source material. The authors of the canonical gospels "just made up" new gospels from existing gospels. Canonization is the rule *not to do* what the writers of the canonized gospels *did*. Can we make new gospels? Well, Matthew, Mark, Luke, and John all did.

That we *can* make up new gospels is shown us, then, by existing gospels, all of which were themselves made up. That we *should* make up new gospels follows from another contradiction of canonization: the sacralizing of a gospel that bears the gdwd travesties the gdwd that the gospel bears. Canonization *makes* the good news equivalent of the bad news mistake that "Don't shoot the messenger" warns against: it venerates the messenger instead of the message. We have another name for this mistake: idolatry. Venerating an idol mistakes the representation for the represented. To keep regarding the representation *as* a representation *of* the represented, not to mistake it for the represented itself, the representation cannot be the *only* representation. If *this* golden calf or *this* crucifix *is* the deity, then I've made the substitution error: I'm venerating the representation itself in place of what it represents. Multiplying representations averts the error: only if this crucifix and also this one and this one, and also this stick and this bit of eggshell and this chip of green sea glass, all can represent the represented have they retained their role as representations, without assuming the place of the represented. Multiply gospels, then, to avoid venerating a gospel in place of the gdwd it represents.

In at least this way, gdwd resembles music: it has no predetermined, fixed limits. No four songs exhaust music, no matter how wonderful the songs in question. Even if I have really great taste and deep knowledge, and have chosen four exceptionally marvelous songs, if I think those songs exhaust music—if I think they're the only "real" songs—my concept of music is inadequate. Analogously, no four gospels exhaust gdwd.

Let there be more songs. Let there be more gospels. Here is one more.

Didaskalíai Didáskalou

Could I reiterate even one truth xhe uttered, you would pick up rocks to stone me, and fire would leap from the rocks and consume you.

True teaching is not the teacher's own.

My followers don't follow me.

Those who *don't* see *do* see.

Who hears me hears who I hear.

Drink from my mouth, become me.

Carrying you on my shoulders, I carry what you carry.

Share your breath with other breathers.

Share silence with the silenced.

Freely receive, freely give.

I withdraw from those who advance but I brood over
those who brood.

I speak to the awestruck and I speak through
their speechlessness.

I replace with love the persecution of those who replace
persecution with love.

As spouse embraces spouse, I embrace those who embrace.

As the wedding bed welcomes the wedded, my love
welcomes love.

I reject the rejection of those who reject. I hate the hatred
of the hateful.

Death vomits my torso and limbs. Death cannot digest my face.

In life the living of life lives.

The world is a corpse-eater, eating everything that dies. Truth is a life-eater, so one nourished by truth will not die. The god is a human-eater.

The god is a dyer. Anything dyed with purple turns purple; anyone dyed with immortality becomes immortal.

The god is living, not dead, god of the living, not the dead.

Worship with breath the god who gives breath.

The god who looks at everyone, no one looks at.

Who walks in daylight doesn't stumble; who walks in nightdark does.

Light alternates with darkness. Walk while you have light.

In darkness neither sighted nor sightless sees, but when light shines only one sees what is lit.

Why remain in darkness when you have access to light? Why drink murky water when you have access to clear?

Retain from a full net one keeper; return the rest to the sea.

The one with everything to say finds no one to say it to.

Know the xon, know the fother. Know the xon of humanity, know yourself.

Split a log, find the fother. Lift a rock, find the xon.

The god is *here*, not *there*.

Nothing covered stays undiscovered; nothing concealed remains unknown.

Don't justify yourself to others. The god knows you, and what humans prize the god detests.

When you give to charity, don't let your left hand know your right hand's work. When you pray, close the door to your room. When you fast, brush your hair and wash your face, to conceal from other people what your fother who stays in secrecy and sees the secret sees.

Householder to gardener, of a sterile fig tree: I've waited three years for fruit. Cut it down. Gardener: Boss, let me dig in manure around it. If it bears no fruit next year, *then* cut it down.


A sower sowed seed. Some fell onto the path and birds ate it. Some fell on rocky ground, sprouted quickly in shallow soil, got sun-scorched, and withered. Some fell among thistles that choked it out. What fell onto rich soil, though, grew, spread, and gave grain, a hundred times what had been sown.

A pearl loses no value in mud, gains none by being rubbed with balsam. A child of the god is not less precious wrapped in rags, or more precious ensembled in silk.

Workers deserve their keep.

The slave seeks freedom, not the slaveholder's holdings.

Now you dress yourself and go where you please, but soon you'll be dressed by others and led where they decide.

The dreamer rules, the ruler sleeps.

Most graced? The servant. The xon of humanity is not served, but serves.

Foxes have dens and birds nests, but the xon of humanity has nowhere to rest.

For life, eat the flesh of the xon of humanity, and drink xher blood.

The xon of humanity covers you more closely even than your clothes.

Don't be duped into searching here or there. The xon of humanity is within you.

By camouflaging bad things with good names, deceivers dupe the free into conformity.

Called a sonofabitch *because* born of the fother and the mather.

Though *god* names the perfect, speaker and hearer conceive an imperfect. Same with *fother, xon, holy breath, life, light, resurrection, church,* . . .

The first *are* last, the last first.

Graced, the gasping for breath: all air is theirs.
Graced, the tearful: their cheeks are already wiped dry.
Graced, the unassuming: the whole earth is theirs.
Graced, the alone: they dwell where they came from and return to.
Graced, those who exist before being born: what is and was will be.
Graced, the one who from the beginning knows the end.
Graced, the hungry and thirsty for justice: they embody it.
Graced, the merciful: mercy secures them.
Graced, the disposition-detoxed: they glimpse the god.
Graced, the peacemakers: the god recognizes them.
Graced, those punished for their justice: they are justified.

By sound eyes a whole body is lit, by clouded eyes dimmed.

What pairs breath with light sends emissaries to us, the lit.

Unity illuminates, division darkens.

To have light, find a *source* of light.

Speculations on cosmic scale and measurements of cosmic distances miss this: infinite light is truth, and gives truth.

We inhabit a limitless medium that not even emissaries can measure, an infinite breath no eye can see, no mind comprehend, no name designate.

Call it the fother, but remember: what is is infinite, incomprehensible, imperishable, singular, eternal, graceful, unknown but self-knowing, immeasurable, unrepresentable, blessed and blessing.

Anyone with ears for the infinite, listen.

Attend what no eye sees, no ear hears, no hand touches, no mind comprehends.

One borrower owed five hundred, another owed fifty. Neither could pay, so the lender forgave both debts.

A parent of two children told both to do their chores. One child said *I won't*, but later did; the other said *I will*, but didn't. Of the two, which respected the parent?

In a place of worship, a deacon stood at the front and prayed, thanking the god that he was not like other people: thieves, cheaters, or adulterers. I fast twice a week, he insisted, and I donate a tenth of my income. A broker stood to the side, and looked down. He beat his breast and prayed, God, be merciful toward my errancy. Only one returned home absolved.

Without making right left and left right and up down and before after, you do not inhabit the medium of the god.


Make two one, inside outside, and above below; make male and female one, so that male is not male and female is not female. *Then you will inhabit the medium of the god.*


If the medium of the god were the sky, birds would precede you; if it were the sea, then fish. In fact the medium is within you.


*Look, here is the medium of the god! Look, there it is!* No, find the medium of the god within yourself.

No one who, hand to plow, looks back inhabits the medium
of the god.


Sooner a camel through the eye of a needle than a wealthy person
into the medium of the god.


Reconsider, for the medium of the god surrounds you.


Some were born queer, some became queer, and some queered
themselves to inhabit the medium of the god.


The medium of the fother need not *arrive*: it includes
the earth already.

The medium of the god, a minuscule mustard seed grown into the largest herb, spreads such broad leaves that birds nest in its shade.

The medium of the fother: meal from a broken jar, spilled out along the road behind the bearer who didn't realize until arriving home that the jar was empty.

The medium of the god, an ear of wheat that sprouted, ripened, and scattered its seed, filling the field with next season's wheat.

The medium of the fother is leaven mixed into meal, a few pinches plenty for the whole.

Pray like this: Hear us, fother, as you hear your xon,
from the sky illuminate earth with your luster.
Give us today bread for today.
Forgive of our indebtedness what we forgive of others'.
Turn us toward nurture and away from harmfulness.

Praise like this: over-fother, beyond naming or observing,
your wholeness gives off light brighter than goldgleam.
Your word solicits reconsideration and tenders life.
You are the clarity and calm of the solitary.
You see us as chooser sees chosen,
you breathe into us the breath for which we gasp.

Error does not *exist*, you *enact* it.

Don't make rules beyond parameters the god has imposed, as if you were the lawgiver.

Throw a stone at one who has erred, if you yourself never have.

Don't judge by appearances, or to keep up appearances; judge with just judgment.

The judgment you judge with judges you; the measure you measure with measures you.

Life is not enriched by riches.

What profit, acquiring the whole world, paying with the soul? How buy back one's soul?

Cache only what neither moth nor rust erases, what no thief can steal.

The land yielded so bountifully that its owner, not having storage for the surplus, wondered what to do, and decided to build bigger barns, to store reserve for many years. But the god questioned the person: Unwise one, on the night your life is demanded of you, who will own this hoard?

No more than one can mount two horses or stretch two bows, can one report both to money and to the god.

Bring something from home to the house of the fother, but take nothing home from it.

Don't make the fother's house a house of commerce.

Don't lend at interest; give to one who can't pay you back.

Not what enters from outside but what originates within corrupts.

Natures, structures, creatures: all exist with one another, through one another.

All those big buildings? Soon enough, not one stone on a stone will stand.

Learn from the one to be one with one another. The fother of all is immeasurable and immutable, ordering mind, word, division, jealousy, and fire, all into one principle, breathing them all with one breath.

Good, bad, life, death: each dissolves, but what informs the world is indissoluble and eternal.

No fractured structure stands.

Where two or three commune, the xon of humanity
is their communion.

What the god has united, let no human divide.

Of fire-formed vessels, glass and ceramic, only the glass,
breath-shaped, can be remade after being broken.

I separate you out, one from a thousand, two from ten thousand,
to join you together.

A householder returned from a long journey to settle accounts with those to whom he had entrusted his holdings. The first came forward, saying, Boss, you gave me five thousand; look, I've made five thousand more. The householder said, Well done. The next said, Boss, you gave me two thousand; look, I've made two thousand more. The householder said, Well done. The last said, Boss, I knew that you're a hard man, harvesting what you didn't plant and gathering what you didn't scatter, so from fear I hid your thousand in the ground. Now I return what is yours. The householder replied, At least you should have put my money in the bank, so I'd have it back with interest. He gave that thousand to the one with ten thousand.

Faith receives, love gives.

Love makes of many one.

Faith, earth; hope, water; love, air; knowledge, light.

Love your sibling as you love your soul, protect your sibling as you protect your own eyes.

No greater love than sharing soul.

Kiss one another in grace.


Be hope to the hopeless, help to the helpless, health to the sick, life to the dead.


Even if you are ill-received, still be receptive.


Steady the stumbling, treat the sick. Feed the hungry, spell the fatigued.


Slapped on one cheek, turn the other. Sued for your coat, offer also your shirt. Ordered to walk one mile, walk two.

Ask, to receive; seek, to find; knock, for the door to be opened.

Seeker, seek. Find not the found but the finding.

Finding finds disturbance, disturbance disturbs wonder, wonder wonders at oneness.

Who would not leave a whole flock at pasture to search for the one missing sheep?

Truth to tell, the god anticipates the beginning, foretells the will-have-begun.

Truth to tell, flesh is born of flesh, breath born of breath.

Truth to tell, the xon of humanity came up from the earth *and* down from the sky.

Truth to tell, the principals cannot see or detain those drenched in perfect light.

Truth to tell, the living god lives in you as you live in the living god.

Evidences? When I've willed you an inheritance the whole world couldn't hold?

The meanings hidden in these sayings do not die.

Who doesn't heed the writings wouldn't listen even to one risen from the dead.

What you're watching for happened without your noticing.

A wide gate and a broad road lead to destruction, and many enter there. A tight gate and a narrow road lead to life, but few find it.

Guard against the emissaries of impoverishment, the visitants of chaos. Beware the deep sleep, confinement to the inside of the below.

Beware of false prophets, ravenous wolves dressed as sheep.

Emissaries and prophets give you what you have already.

The prophet goes unrecognized among familiars, at home.

Receive a prophet, be a prophet; receive a just person, be just. Give a cup of cool water to one of the belittled, be enlarged.

From the word, truth; from truth, liberation.

The breath of truth guides you to truth, not by speaking for itself but by reporting what it hears.

Take care not to turn torpid from partying, drunkenness, and worries.

Return by the same route. Avoid beastliness.

Be passersby.

Sound sayings breathe and live.

Read the writings. Draw life from their witness.

The word exudes milk, honey, oil, and wine. The word spreads strong roots and bears lush fruit, sustenance from generation to generation, age to age.

One who hears and practices sound principles builds on bedrock: despite rain and wind and rising water, the house will not fall. One who hears but does not heed sound principles doubles the dolt who builds on sand: a little rain, one good gust, and down the house tumbles.

Learn anew from the words you already know.

When you host a dinner, don't invite friends or kin or wealthy neighbors, expecting them to reciprocate. Invite persons who are unhoused or unable to walk or unable to see; then you will be graced, not recompensed but just.

A traveler journeying from Jerusalem to Jericho got robbed, beaten, and left for dead. A passing priest crossed to the other side. As did a Levite. But a Samaritan bandaged the traveler's wounds, salving them with oil and wine, and brought the person to an inn and tended the person. The next day, the Samaritan gave the innkeeper money and said, Take care of this person, and whatever more it costs you I'll repay when I return.

Lose the world to find the medium of the god; take a sabbath from the sabbath to meet the fother.

The sabbath exists for humans, not humans for the sabbath.

What is forbidden on the sabbath? To do good? To preserve life?

If you are laying a gift at the altar but just then remember that your sibling holds a grudge against you, drop your gift and go; first reconcile with your sibling, *then* offer your gift.

Figure it out: *the god favors mercy over sacrifice.*

A human with hidden intestines lives, but one with exposed intestines dies. A tree with hidden roots grows and leafs out, but expose its roots and the tree withers.

What is within you gives life. What is not within you has killed you already.

A precious object would hardly be hidden in a precious container. The priceless is more securely kept in the worthless, so soul shelters in body.

The hidden hides before your very eyes.

Unify interior and exterior.

Observe the breath, become breath. Observe the salve, become salve.

The same breath that stokes the fire blows it out.

See truth in yourself as you see yourself in water.

Distracted by your own likeness, you miss what does not insist on being seen.

Know everything except yourself, know nothing.

Be first and last. Be honored and scorned.

Be promiscuous and chaste, spouse and virgin, the doula who eases both birth and death.

Be the silence that soaks up speech, and the foresight made of memory.

Be the voice with various timbres and the voiced with various inflections.

Be the assignment of your own name. Be knowledge and ignorance.

Be caution and daring, security and terror, war and peace.

Be godless, as your worship of the godliest god.

Be the one you've dismissed but can't forget.

Be the one from whom you hide and the one to whom you show yourself.

Be the peace for which war is declared. Be alien and citizen.

Be restraint and the unrestrained, conviction and acquittal, urge and self-control.

Be the unspeaking source of the spoken.

Be the one who cries out, and be the one who hears the cry.

Study death: its teachings all prove true.

Vultures convene over the corpse.

Deference to the dead dismisses the living.

Death and life, both on offer; one choosing between them has chosen.

Death cannot live, life cannot die.

If you fear the flesh, it will terrorize you.

Don't exploit weakness, don't fear power.

Anger fosters fear; fear feeds anger.

If you fear what looms over you, it will swallow you. Look within. Let words root you to earth. Over the fearless there can be no tyranny, no tyrant.

Fire with nothing to burn extinguishes itself.

Murderers of the body can't kill the soul.

The body weeps, weighted; the mind laughs, weightless.

Don't fret what to eat, what to wear. Isn't health more than cuisine, fitness more than fashion? Birds don't plant or harvest or gather into barns, yet the fother feeds them. Don't you matter as much? Who by worry can add one day to a lifespan? And why worry over clothes? Lilies don't spin or weave, but even Solomon in his splendor never dressed as well. Let others crave what your fother knows you need. Seek the medium of the god and xher justice; all else follows.

Two who make peace have moved a very mountain.

Making peace gives peace.

Give peace, receive peace.

Peace suffuse you. Joy and grace and fortitude fill you, displacing fear.

The harmful cannot harm you. Be at peace.

Xher words open to the skies.

www.ingramcontent.com/pod-product-compliance
Lightning Source LLC
Chambersburg PA
CBHW061252040426
42444CB00010B/2358